Advance Praise for
The Future Is Trust

"Trust is a choice. It's not the easy path, but it's the one that matters. Lisa and Rick share a generous and powerful manifesto that can help us get there."
— Seth Godin, founder, altMBA

"This is a thoroughly motivating overview of the power of trust to shape our relationships and organizations. This is a perfect book for anyone who wants to understand trust better, develop trust-centered skills, heal from trust issues, and get better at developing trust in their personal and professional relationships."
— Kat Vellos, speaker and author of *We Should Get Together: The Secret to Cultivating Better Friendships*

"Trust is the invisible currency of success and wellbeing. Its role is heightened in a world with increasing interactions between humans, machines and systems, and their creators. Lisa and Rick provide a convincing case and a thought-provoking guide on trust."
— Vijay Kasireddy, Partner Director of Engineering, Microsoft

"A must read for every leader to understand the what, why and how of trust. Rick and Lisa will show you how to turn trust into a competitive advantage. Highly recommended."
— Eric Moeller, Director of Product Marketing, Sage and author of *Levelling Up: The Complete Guide to Starting a Mastermind Group*

"Trust is the bottom line. Thanks to global leadership consultants Rick and Lisa, you now have the thinking and tools to build trust in yourself, within your team, and for your brand. You can't afford to miss this book."
— Louise Karch, Bestselling Author of *Word Glue*

"Trust. Is. Everything (hard stop!) Once you understand the internal and external levers of building trust, you can start to check in with yourself, asking: Am I being intentional about extending and earning it? Lisa and Rick cut through the BS of your typical leadership book to provide a concise, pragmatic, and action-oriented take on a highly nuanced subject."
— Brodie Wasserman, Manager of Integrated Strategy, WarnerMedia (Bleacher Report)

"Trust is an underappreciated and undervalued asset. It can be mined to depletion like a finite resource, or cultivated like a renewable one that grows as it fuels human endeavor. Lisa and Rick get this, and crafted an approach to earning and employing trust that leaders can leverage to make a meaningful and sustainable impact. If you seek to make meaningful change happen, trust is the way, and this book will help."

— Scott Perry, Chief Difference-Maker, Creative on Purpose and Bestselling Author of *Onward*

"Trust is everything, yet we often take it for granted - that is until we need it most. Not only do Rick and Lisa present a compelling human and business case for leaders to invest in building trust, they also provide a practical and transformative approach to doing so."

— Oni Blackstock, MD, MHS, Founder and Executive Director, Health Justice

"Trust is not static. We are always moving either toward or away from trust. Rick and Lisa generously share their expertise in digestible insights on how to make becoming and staying trusted a daily practice."

— Shannon Weber, MSW, Author of *Show Up Hard: A Road Map For Helpers In Crisis*

"If you understand the powerful role relationships play in your life - personal and professional - then you'll surely have felt the joy of experiencing trusting relationships and the endless possibilities for expansion, learning and growth those relationships open up for you. And if you're human, you'll also know the confusion, complexity and pain mistrust can breed in relationships and the opportunities that are lost as a result. This book is a simple, trustworthy and actionable framework and guide for anyone who wants to become more trusting and more trustworthy. Read it. Do it. Trust me, you'll be glad you did."

— Rebecca Kirstein Resch, CEO, Inqli

"If Austin Kleon and Seth Godin's books had a baby it would be The Future is Trust. A digestible and thought-provoking book that packs a punch. If you're a leader looking to understand, practice, and cultivate trust in your team or organization this is the book for you."

— Peter Shepherd, Director and Founder, Human Periscope and Co-host of The Long and the Short of It podcast

"The Future Is Trust by Lisa Lambert and Rick Kitagawa is deceptively short, because it delivers a powerful message about the core of human relationships. The authors waste no time or space in getting to the core of why Trust is so essential in our workplace and society today, and more importantly, how to earn it. We are social creatures by nature, incapable of living without meaningful interactions with one another, and at the core of the effectiveness of those interactions, small or monumental, is Trust. Take the hour to read this book and consider your own relationship with trust, it is well worth your time."

— Stacy Slattery Richards, JD, Owner and CEO, OysterReef Coaching

"In legacy organizations, the coin of the realm is power. In collaborative networks, the coin of the realm is trust. If you find yourself in a legacy organization desperately moving toward agile, adaptive, network-like structures, Rick and Lisa can show you why trust matters, and how to gain a capacity for building it."

— Steve Frost, Executive Director/Cartographer of the Future, The Tasai Collective

"Having been in situations where trust was lacking, I can say that trust truly is a critical resource on which everything, literally everything, is based. Trust seems really ephemeral and intangible, but Rick and Lisa not only show us how real it is, but also provide a practical way forward towards building and repairing it. If you learn to build trust, you can learn to build anything."

— Graham Ballachey, Vice President of Engineering, American Lithium Corp.

"Trust is a defining issue of our time and a way forward toward a more productive world. Lisa and Rick present a pragmatic and actionable framework for earning, extending, strengthening, and restoring trust in individuals, teams, and organizations. The Future Is Trust reminds us that people are the foundation of companies, organizations, and communities."

—Diena Lee Mann, VP Product, SoundCommerce

"We know that trust is the foundation of any successful relationship, both personally and professionally. But how do we build trust as individuals, teams, and organizations? This practical and actionable book is your roadmap for how to earn, extend, strengthen, and even restore trust. While you'd wish you had read it sooner, you'll be able to put its lessons into action immediately."

—Brent Lamphier, Founder, EQmethod

"Now more than ever trust is needed in every organization, relationship and interaction. We have seen what happens without it and it doesn't end well. Lisa and Rick do an incredible job breaking trust down and providing you with the understanding and tools required to level up. This is now required reading for our whole team."
—Jenna Watson-Brawn, VP of Sales, Motive.io

"Using a combination of data, real world insights and actionable frameworks, Lisa and Rick have created a go-to reference for leaders who know the value of trust. Trust gets results. In both our professional and personal lives. This book is a quick start guide, and must read, for any new leader. And a great refresher for seasoned leaders."
—Tia Newcomer, Board Member and Life Science Executive

"In today's challenging world, there's nothing more valuable than trust. The Future is Trust gets to the core of this reality, laying out tangible actions we can all take to grow and cultivate this invaluable asset."
— Sean Lee, Head of External Relations, TRIUMF

"We live in an era where fake-news, deep fakes and AI will turn trust into a scarce and valuable asset. Lisa and Rick's book will give you a clear path to build that asset by developing trusting relationships at small and large scales with your audience and collaborators so you can cultivate resilience and propel your organisation forward."
— Jaime Arredondo, Founder, Bold and Open and Board Member, Open Lande

"The Future is Trust is like a looking glass to this precious virtue. Perfect for those seeking to find the treasure of trust and willing to be present to find it. Heart by heart, step by step, community by community—a kind and just world is possible."
— KellyAnn Romanych, Deputy Executive Director, Veterans Legal Institute

"The book that will convince anyone that trust is the highest value leadership asset."
— Eduardo Gomez Ruiz, UX Research Lead, Miro and Associate Professor, IE Business School

Moose & Monster Press

Design and layout by Rick Kitagawa + Lisa Lambert.
Proofread by Al Gilliom.

Jetpack People Illustrations by Abiyyu Suryowibisono.

Library of Congress Cataloging-in-Publication Data is available.

ISBN 978-1-7776399-0-7

For more information about special discounts for bulk, non-profit, or educational orders, please contact: thefutureistrust@spotlighttrust.com

First Printing, June 2021
10 9 8 7 6 5 4 3 2 1

THE FUTURE IS

TRUST

Embracing the Era of
Trust-Centered Leadership

Rick Kitagawa & Lisa Lambert

For the people who have trusted us along the way,
including YOU.

Table of Contents

Act III - How to Build Trust

Epilogue

If we can learn to trust one another more, we can have unprecedented human progress.

—Frances Frei

Prologue

Choosing to adapt to a new era.

The future can be really different than we ever imagined. The future can come to be much sooner than we ever imagined.

We've all recently experienced this firsthand. As decades happened in days throughout 2020 and into early 2021, the pandemic and social reckonings slingshotted our global civilization forward at warp-speed into a new era and there is no going back.

There is only forward—to a new, more complex, and forever uncertain future that is currently presenting leaders with an opportunity to make a pivotal choice:

- Become irrelevant: Leaders can choose to carry on as if the world hasn't fundamentally changed and watch the cracks in our traditional systems continue to grow until they eventually crumble.

- Adapt: Leaders can choose to learn crucial lessons from our past and intentionally design this new era in ways that work for all, and not just a select few, so that together we can collectively enjoy unprecedented human progress.

The leaders, organizations, and communities we work with at our consultancy Spotlight Trust are those choosing to adapt and design this new era. By choosing to adapt, they've also made the choice to embrace the most valuable leadership asset of our time and the currency of this new era: trust.

Accumulating and investing in the currency of trust requires a shift in power dynamics from power over to power with: control and fear (power over) are inversely related to trust (power with). The leaders, organizations, and communities that will thrive moving forward are those who come to grips with letting go of control so they can fully embrace trust—the most valuable currency for human connection, building resiliency, and navigating uncertainty.

LEADERSHIP IS CHANGING

Power dynamics are shifting from command-and-control to **trust**.

OLD ERA

- Work is transactional
- Power over
- Fitting in
- White supremacy and discrimination
- Patriarchal
- Conformity
- Exclusion
- Oppression
- Hierarchy and siloization
- Short-term results

CURRENCY = CONTROL + FEAR

NEW ERA

- Work is relational
- Power with
- Belonging
- Anti-racism and equity
- Participatory
- Diversity
- Inclusion
- Liberation
- Networks and dynamic collaboration
- Lasting, meaningful impact

CURRENCY = TRUST

RICK KITAGAWA & LISA LAMBERT - 3

The leaders, organizations, and communities that will flourish in our fast-changing world are those who acknowledge what's essentially at the core of the future of work. The future of work isn't about the growing adoption of technologies like artificial intelligence (AI), machine learning, and robotics in the workplace. Nor is it about the changing physical distribution of the workforce. The future of work is ultimately about redefining the very nature of work itself: work isn't transactional, it's relational—and relationships all come down to trust.

This redefinition requires a reimagination of the systems that make up workplaces. It requires new ways of thinking about organizational structures, skill sets, and mindsets for a new era. It requires new ways of thinking about leadership. It requires hard work, making space for nuance, and an openness to experimentation and learning.

It requires leaders like YOU to make the choice to adapt. It requires leaders like YOU to embrace the era of Trust-Centered Leadership and commit to working together to design a better world for all.

This book is meant to help you do just that.

● ● ● ● ● ● ● ● ● ● ●

**Organizations are no longer
built on force, but on trust.**

—Peter Drucker

Trust, defined.

We all have firsthand experience with trust, but what does trust really mean?

Before we go further, let's get aligned on what we're talking about.

Here's our definition of trust:

Trust is a noun and a verb.

Trust is a placement of confidence that stems from a combination of a willingness to be vulnerable and to actively engage with the unknown.

Trust involves taking a risk and dancing with uncertainty, with the belief that you'll be better for it, though a positive outcome isn't guaranteed. That's why it's "trust" and not "a sure thing."

Often, the fear associated with uncertainty, risk, and lack of guarantee is what stands in the way of building trust. Overcoming that fear is essential to building a more trustworthy and trusted world: one where we all enjoy higher quality connections, are treated with dignity and respect, and have an equal opportunity to thrive.

We need leaders like you to be brave and lead by example by extending and earning trust. We need you to be Trust-Centered leaders. This book shares our practical framework to do just that.

Please join us on our mission to build a more trustworthy and trusted world, together.

In a world turned upside-down, all who run organizations, all who seek deeper relationships, all who want more meaning in their lives would do well to consider trust as the asset they most desire.

—David W. Checketts

Act I - Why Trust

Trust is the defining issue of our time.

All day, we navigate a complex world filled with overwhelming amounts of misinformation, disinformation, half-truths, delusions, selfishness, and flat-out lies.

The internet has been the great equalizer for many. It's given everyday people the ability to readily connect beyond their physical geographies and access the same information as deep subject matter experts with years of experience. Knowledge is out there for anyone to grab, and people can start a business with little more than a web browser and a dream.

With increased access, more and more people are looking to make their unique contribution to the world.

Never before has trust been so important in moving our world forward and making change happen.

Whether it's enrolling someone in your vision on a personal level, empowering a team, driving policy at a national level, or tackling complex global challenges like climate change, everything comes down to trust.

Trust in yourself. Trust with another. Trust at scale.

No one will support your big, audacious goal if you don't trust yourself to verbalize it.

No one will care about your cure for cancer if they don't trust you and your development process.

No one will hire you if they don't trust you and your ability to deliver value for their endeavor.

No one will invest in your business if they don't trust in your team or your ability to create value and generate return on investment.

No one will implement your plan to change your organization if you can't build trust with the relevant stakeholders.

When trust is strong, anything is possible.

Trust - are you intentional about extending and earning it?

Building trust is one of the most critical challenges facing our society today.

—Frances Hesselbein

Without trust, we go nowhere.

You can't transform your full potential into lasting success without trust.

You might be driven by a clear purpose, but without trust—trust in yourself, trust in another, and trust at scale—you won't reach your aim.

You might have all the supporting evidence in your favor, but any interaction or exchange comes down to one simple question:

Do you trust one another?

Clearly, without self-trust you can't have organizational trust, and without the latter no real achievement.

—Michael H. Jordan

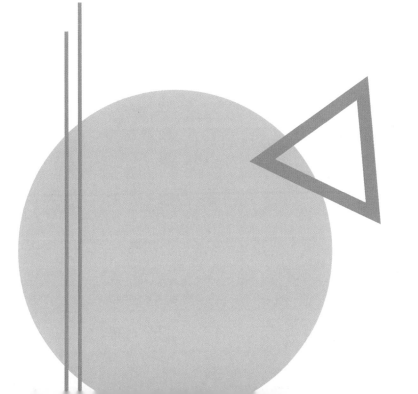

A lack of trust is expensive.

Low trust costs us in many ways.

When trust is low, we pay a penalty in terms of transaction costs, time, red tape, bureaucracy, suspicion, second-guessing, organizational debt, internal politics, employee turnover, litigation, frustration, misunderstanding, low morale, and poor performance.

Oh yes, it can also cost us our relationships, communities, customers, sales, partnerships, jobs, and, in some cases, even our lives and the lives of others.

Can you really afford not to invest in building trust?

Leaders tend to overestimate trust.

Most of us think that we're highly trustworthy and that others trust us. After all, why wouldn't they?

Unfortunately, often we can be too close to the subject and be unable to see or acknowledge the truth. No one likes to admit they're not trusted.

A 2017 global workplace study[1] asked 1675 leaders and staff members in 95 countries to score the phrase, "Leaders here are sincere," which is highly correlated with trust. The results showed that leaders' overestimated their own level of trustworthiness by about 21% over the average front line employee.

Regardless of your intentions, a lack of trust can be the fly in the soup that spoils the whole pot.

As a leader, it's critical not to take trust for granted.

●　　●　　●　　●　　●

Mistrust doubles the cost of doing business.

—John Whitney

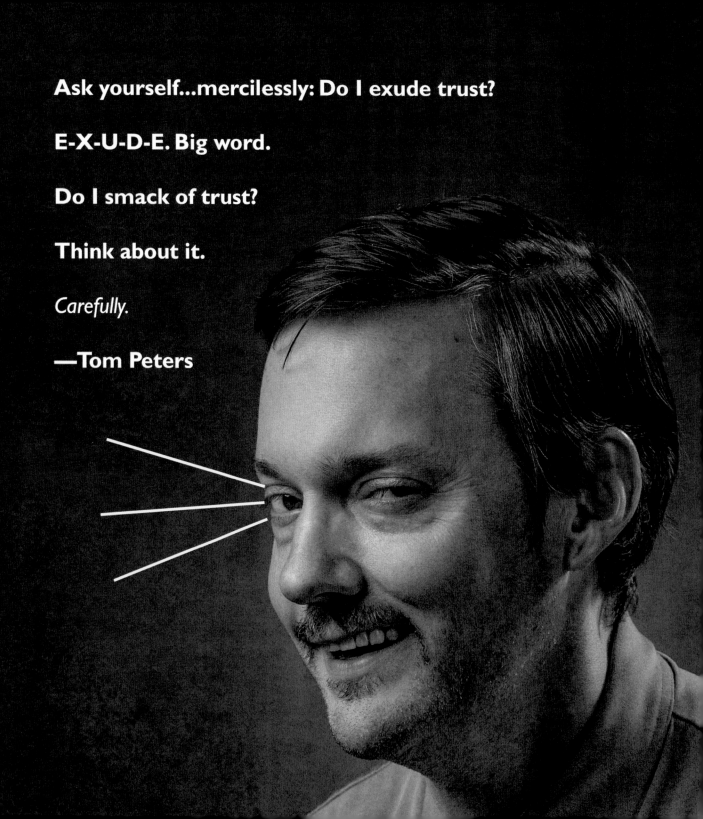

Ask yourself...mercilessly: Do I exude trust?

E-X-U-D-E. Big word.

Do I smack of trust?

Think about it.

Carefully.

—Tom Peters

Low trust is dysfunctional.

Think of a time where you perceived trust was low. This could be in a conversation, a meeting, working on a project, etc.

What did you notice?

How did you feel?

When we've asked these questions to hundreds of leaders from around the world, here are some of the most common responses they've shared:

- Difficult to make progress
- Low productivity
- High anxiety
- People hoard information
- Cutthroat and competitive
- People don't share ideas and feedback
- People act defensive
- Morale is low
- People feel invisible or actively hide
- Things are stuck
- People feel frustrated
- It's exhausting
- Lack of transparency
- People feel small
- Feeling of elephants in the room
- People feel isolated
- Feeling of walking on eggshells
- Lack of connection
- Things move slowly, yet with little patience
- People are disengaged

A space without trust is a space where nothing goes well.

Lack of trust within an organization saps its energy, fosters a climate of suspicion and second-guessing, completely devastates teamwork and replaces it with internal politics.

The end result is low morale and the consequent low standards of performance.

—Koh Boon Hwee

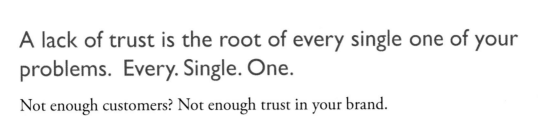

A lack of trust is the root of every single one of your problems. Every. Single. One.

Not enough customers? Not enough trust in your brand.

High employee turnover? There's not enough trust in your culture, leadership, and/or vision.

Feeling underpaid? Didn't get that promotion you wanted? Not enough trust in the perceived commercial value you bring, whether or not that judgment is true.

When you solve for trust, everything gets better.

Professional and personal, it all comes down to trust.

Trust is the glue that bonds great people, processes, and environments, and ensures long-term success. If this critical component is missing, everything else falls apart.

—Rita Bailey

The trade-off in not trusting people as the default is, as far as I'm concerned, a far more painful path.

—Rebecca Kirstein Resch

But low trust can also be strategic.

It's important that we trust in who and what is trustworthy.

Choosing not to extend trust can be a resilience strategy.

For example, you might reject a job offer because you don't trust that the organization's values align with your own and that the leadership team is truly invested in its people's success. Or you might steer clear of working with a potential supplier for your business because you don't trust that they can deliver.

If you've experienced a breach of trust in the past, distrust can be a viable strategy to avoid future breaches.

But this strategy must be used judiciously, as choosing not to extend trust is oftentimes an incredibly limiting decision.

The tight, defensive shell you'll create for yourself will wall you into a lonely, confined, and ineffective place. Choosing not to trust as your default is choosing to blind yourself to new opportunities and build barriers to connection, communication, and collaboration.

Breach trust at your own risk.

Humanity is more connected than ever and breaching trust can burn bridges. It can also be a death sentence if you do it enough times.

Anyone familiar with the story of Elizabeth Holmes[2], the now disgraced ex-CEO of Theranos[3], understands how damaging breaking trust is. Besides the $500,000 fine and ruined reputation, Holmes now faces 12 felony counts of fraud and up to 20 years in prison for making false claims to investors, doctors, and patients about the effectiveness of their blood testing technology.

When you breach trust, you're playing with fire.

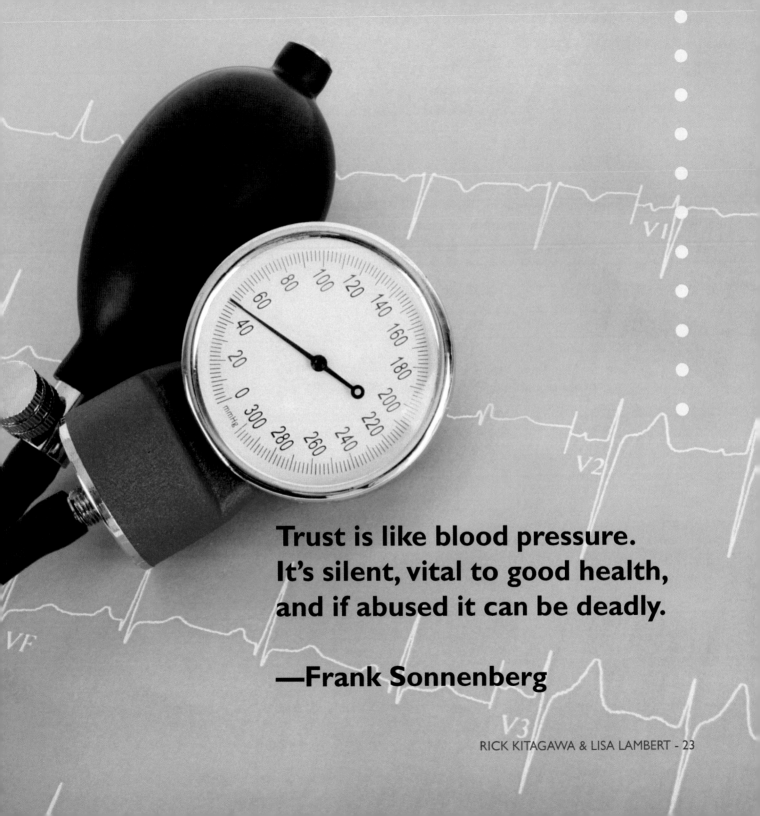

Trust is like blood pressure.
It's silent, vital to good health,
and if abused it can be deadly.

—Frank Sonnenberg

RICK KITAGAWA & LISA LAMBERT - 23

Restoring trust is delicate work and not always possible.

In our consulting practice, we often get asked how to repair trust: the best way to repair trust is to not break it in the first place.

If it's too late for prevention, know that there is no surefire way to restore broken trust. It requires work on your part to become trustworthy and rebuild trust. It also requires forgiveness, understanding, and empathy on the part of the other party with whom you're seeking to restore trust. As with all things that depend on others, there are no guarantees.

We like to think about repairing trust as being analogous to the Japanese art of kintsugi, or golden joinery, where broken ceramics are repaired with a lacquer mixed with precious metals like gold or platinum. It's a form that acknowledges the damage as part of the ceramic's history, and this act of taking ownership of the damage caused is crucial to the process of rebuilding trust.

That said, unfortunately, some broken ceramics are damaged beyond repair.

Trust is fragile. That is why it can be easily broken and is difficult to repair.

—Richard Massafra

High trust is liberating.

Now think of a time where you perceived trust was high.

What did you notice?

How did you feel?

How do you think others felt?

When we've asked these questions to hundreds of leaders from around the world, here are some of the most common responses they've shared:

- It's highly productive
- People feel safe
- Creativity abounds
- Innovation happens
- Collaboration feels easy
- Team members generously support one another
- People are brave
- It's fun!
- People feel like they matter and their contributions matter
- Respect is high
- Everyone feels included and appreciated
- People feel acknowledged
- People listen and feel listened to
- People feel cared for
- People feel like they belong
- There is camaraderie
- Rapid decision-making
- People feel valued
- It's energizing

High trust creates an abundance of possibilities.

You can't have success without trust. The word trust embodies almost everything you can strive for that will help you succeed.

—Jim Burke

Trust is transformative.

You positively influence the environment when you operate with trust.

Trust converts transactions into relationships.

Trust can change a zero-sum game where there is a winner and a loser into an infinite game where everyone wins. Trust enables cooperation.

One of the most empowering things you can do is trust in yourself.

Trust can transform command-and-control leadership dynamics into generous, caring, collaborative ones where everyone benefits. There's an inverse relationship between the need to control and trust.

Trust is essential to building and maintaining psychological safety and promoting learning behaviors which propel the most effective teams[4].

Trust makes organizations run smoother, more efficiently, and more effectively.

We all want to experience high trust in our interactions and environments. These high-trust settings enable us to show up as our best selves and to do our best work. These settings enable us to be better together.

We need leaders like you to help create high-trust settings.

It feels invisible most of the time, and then you see what a group of people can do when there is trust and it becomes less invisible. It's like 'Huh. That's what trust is. That's how trust shows up.'

—Marie Schacht

Trust is everything.

Trust isn't just a track record of excellence, case studies, logos, and five-star reviews and ratings.

It's all this and more.

Trust is the congruence of all these puzzle pieces. It's how they fit together at every touch point and interaction to create a cohesive experience.

Holes in the trust puzzle are often visible when we find ourselves pulling back—whether it's second-guessing a potential new hire following mediocre reference checks or getting cold feet about a business deal after the potential partner continuously isn't forthright in providing their financial records in the due diligence process.

Trust is the intangible asset that can help assure the long-term sustainability of any organization or enterprise.

—William G. Parrett

And trust changes everything.

Trust is the glue, lubricant, and accelerant to human connection. Trust impacts business results, organizational alignment, innovation, brand, employee engagement, customer relationships, and stakeholder confidence.

Trust is the one thing that changes everything. It provides the leverage needed to create the conditions necessart to change the world.

Trust is the lubrication that makes it possible for organizations to work.

—Warren Bennis

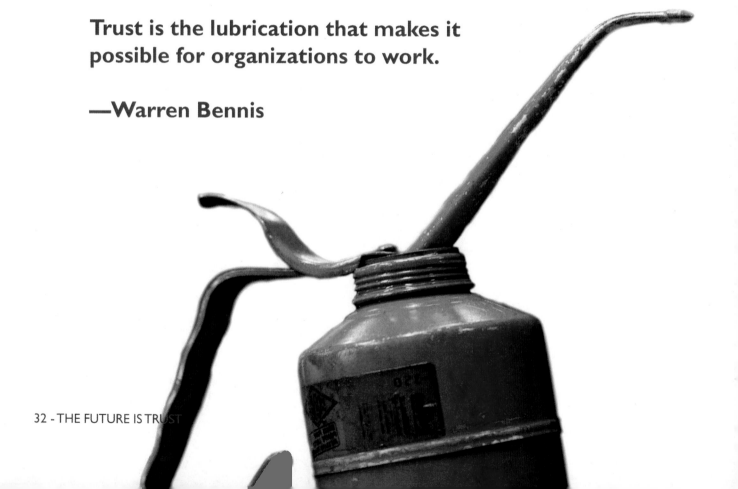

Work isn't transactional, it's relational.

Relationships are all about trust. Trust is the thread that stitches people and our social fabric together. You can have all the procedures and processes in the world, but without trust, your team or operation is going nowhere.

Micromanaging, withholding information or resources, cutthroat corporate ladder climbing, sabotage—these are all symptoms of low-trust cultures.

The remedy that accelerates work: investing in trusted and personalized relationships.

In life and business, relationships are important but they are empty unless they are established and based upon trust.

Trust is the fundamental building block for a brand, and it is the glue for any lasting relationship.

—Horst H. Schulze

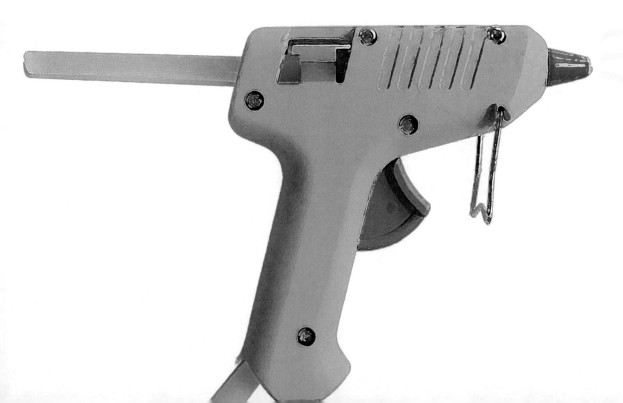

Technical skills are needed, but not sufficient.

Work requires technical skills—no one is disputing that people need hard skills in order to get their jobs done. But technical skills on their own are not enough to succeed and thrive; they're merely the buy-in.

For workplaces and communities to thrive, members need to develop and practice tactical soft skills or, as we call them, Trust-Centered skills.

Trust-Centered skills, along with mindsets[5], are crucial to cultivating high-trust cultures. This potent combination is instrumental in creating the conditions for true, equitable, and lasting change to happen.

Trust-Centered skills are tactical and practical skills we can practice and get better at in order to enroll others in the change we want to make, whether at the micro (one-to-one), mezzo (small groups), or macro (organizational or societal) level.

We know that while sound evidence is crucial, facts and figures—for the most part—don't change people's minds. Emotions, narratives, and beliefs do. There is a reason why there's the popular saying that we do business with those we know, like, and trust.

Technical skills will help get you a seat at the table and earn credibility. Coupled with mindset, Trust-Centered skills give you the prowess to harness the collective power of your organization and community to build inclusive teams with a shared purpose that make a difference, not just groups of humans working around one another.

You might even find that developing your Trust-Centered skills gives you more opportunities to apply your technical skills.

THE THREE LEVELS OF CHANGE

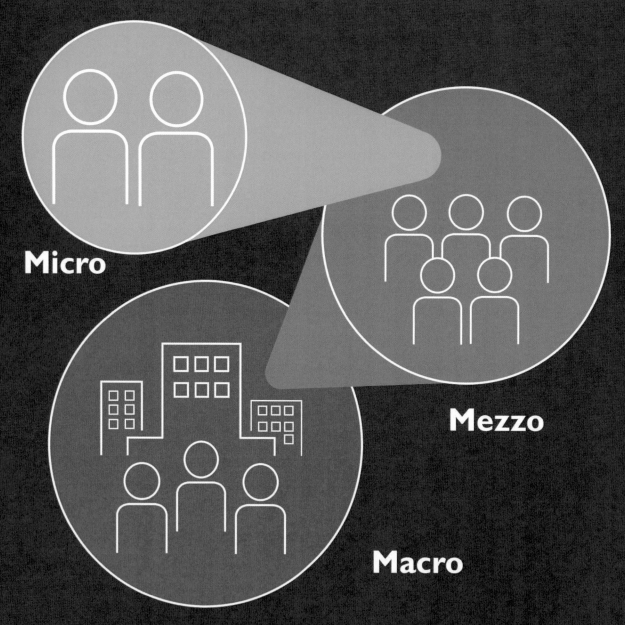

Micro

Mezzo

Macro

As you go to work,
your top responsibility
should be to build trust.

—Robert Eckert

You can develop Trust-Centered skills.

Developing your Trust-Centered skillset is an investment in your sustainable success. Trust-Centered skills include:

- Attention and focus
- Bravery
- Coachability
- Charisma
- Compassion
- Conflict management
- Continuous improvement
- Co-creating spaces of belonging
- Collaboration
- Communication
- Critical thinking
- Curiosity
- Decision-making
- Delegation
- Empathy
- Facilitation
- Generosity
- Giving and receiving feedback well
- Grit
- Humility
- Kindness
- Including and unleashing others
- Initiative
- Integrity
- Listening
- Negotiation
- Non-judgment
- Overcoming impostor syndrome
- Prioritization
- Problem-solving
- Project management
- Resilience
- Selling
- Setting and honoring boundaries
- Storytelling
- Understanding bias
- Understanding value
- Vulnerability

Does this feel like a long list? Well it is: Trust-Centered skills are everything.

In many cultures, there's a lot of talk of "natural born leaders," but leadership isn't a birthright. Anyone can choose to learn and move into a posture of leadership by developing and practicing the skills of great leaders. If you look closely you'll notice that great leaders across history and cultures have something in common: they demonstrate a robust Trust-Centered skill set.

Just like "hard skills," Trust-Centered skills like vulnerability, curiosity, empathy, compassion, and charisma can all be learned if you are willing to do the work to stretch yourself and practice them with others.

After all, trust is relational.

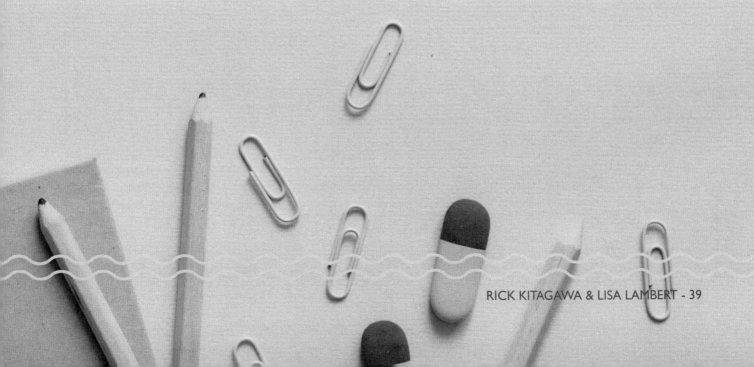

Trust is elemental...it's something that not only has to be talked about and examined but demonstrated every day.

—Stacy Richards

Trust is mission-critical to organizations and communities.

Without trust, you have a collection of people, not a community.

All human interactions are about relationships. Since relationships are all about trust, it's the master key to humans interacting, innovating, and collaborating.

Organizations and communities also need leaders, like you, in order to operate. And guess what leaders need in order to get their jobs done?

Earn trust, earn trust, earn trust.
Then you can worry about the rest.

—Seth Godin

Trust is the highest value leadership asset.

What makes up great organizations and communities? Great people and great leaders.

Leadership is not about title, authority, hierarchy, or brute force. Leadership is not about building followers.

Leadership is about embodying a posture of helping other leaders build trust in and empower themselves to lead. They in turn help others build trust in and empower themselves, and so on, and so on.

This is the highest form of trusting others. It's also a posture you have to choose to move into and is a choice you have to make over and over again.

You can see how important leadership is; how it ripples out with exponential effects.

You can choose to send out ripples into the world that build up others or ones that tear others down.

Choose to be a Trust-Centered Leader. We need you.

Act II - What is Trust?

Trust is a noun and a verb.

If we want to enjoy trust, the noun, and the qualities of high-trust cultures, we need to practice trust, the verb.

This means you need to put in the work of building trust.

It's actually a deeply brave and courageous act when I choose to trust someone and that just feels so tender talking about it. And if that's true then it's also brave and courageous when someone chooses to trust me.

—Shannon Weber

Trust is not a light switch.

We cannot simply turn on trust when we need it.

Earning, strengthening, extending, and restoring trust are all skills you can build, but not overnight.

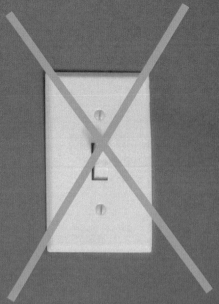

We've all experienced the self-proclaimed 'Super Networker': as soon as they've gotten your name and contact info, they reach out to ask something along the lines of, "Can you do this for me? How about this? Can you introduce me to X? Want to buy this?" There's little trust built up, it's extremely transactional, and it's a complete turn off. No wonder most people shy away from networking events!

Ignore building trust and when you need it most, you'll have the least amount of it. We help those we know, like, and trust, not uncaring, unkind, untrusted strangers who come across as being all about themselves.

Build relationships by focusing on consistently providing meaningful value to others, and continue to nurture and develop these relationships over time.

Trust is built one day at a time, one interaction at a time.

—Frank Ostaseski

Trust is a plant.

Plants need to be attended to and cultivated over time, whether you're planting a seed or tending to a perennial.

It might be tempting to let your attention lax once your plant has built up a hearty root system and is growing big and strong, but if you're not paying attention to it, even the healthiest plant withers.

Trust can be earned, extended, strengthened, and yes, even restored.

Our world mostly works on trust. However, in an era where the baseline of trust is increasingly taken advantage of by people and organizations selling off long-term trust for short-term gain, it's not surprising that younger people in particular are skeptical, weary, and untrusting[6].

So if we want a more trust-filled future, how do we grow and strengthen trust?

Well, we first have to earn it.

We need to put in the work to ensure we're trustworthy and that what we're doing deserves to be trusted. To have trust extended to us, we often have to extend it first. This back-and-forth nature leads to the building and strengthening of trust.

When there is a breach of trust, this delicate interplay is broken. It's much easier to cultivate and strengthen trust than it is to repair it, but restoration can be possible with time and hard work.

It's important to recognize that restoring trust doesn't mean repairing a relationship to its original state. As the art of kintsugi does to an object, the work of restoring trust does to a relationship: mending trust can give a relationship a new lease on life, but that relationship now carries a new story that encapsulates and even exhibits its fractured history. The beauty in the work of restoring trust lies in acknowledging and embracing the possibility of this new story and extending trust anyway while accepting you might not have trust extended back to you.

Trust is an important thing in life, and it can be broken far more easily than it can be gained.

—Lesley Harriot

We're wired for trust.

In many ways, our brains are hardwired for trust. This is why it can be so difficult to trust again following a breach of trust: the breach short-circuited our neurobiology.

A chemical called oxytocin plays a key role in social attachment and affiliation and is our brain's way of signaling trust.

While more robust and rigorous research is needed, oxytocin appears to increase trusting behavior.

Research has shown that in a given situation the amount of oxytocin produced predicted both how much people extend trust to others and how trustworthy they were perceived to be by others[7]. Research has also demonstrated this relationship between oxytocin and trust appears to be universal[8].

Oxytocin increases a person's empathy, an important trait for human connection and collaboration.

This ancient chemical is part of our evolutionary history, and shows how important trust has been to not only our current times but human history as a whole[9].

No matter where you are or who you're working with, establishing trust is at the foundation of working with people.

—Chief Terry Paul

You can measure the benefits of trust.

You can measure trust too, but it might be more useful to measure the benefits of your trust-building efforts.

Measuring the benefits of trust gives you a deep understanding of trust specific to your own context so you can take relevant, practical, and strategic action to level-up trust and improve relations. It also enables you to assess progress in your trust-building efforts, from trusting in yourself, trusting in another, and building trust at scale.

So what benefits of trust can you measure?

Here are just a few examples:

- Increased confidence
- Greater clarity
- Increased operational effectiveness
- Less red tape and bureaucracy
- Higher productivity
- Greater inclusion and sense of belonging
- Increased transparency, accountability, and ownership
- Greater autonomy
- Faster, more-effective decision making

- More engagement
- Less stress and anxiety at work
- Greater idea sharing
- More energy at work
- Fewer sick days
- Less burnout
- Less siloed functions and teams
- Higher performing teams with improved collaboration
- Fewer meetings
- Improved ability to attract and retain top talent

Trust gets results.

Top performing companies are high trust companies.

High trust positively influences communication, cooperation, and information sharing across organizations, boosting productivity[10].

Organizations reported as high trust by their employees beat the average annualized returns of the S&P 500 by a factor of three[11].

Compared with people at low-trust organizations, people at high-trust companies report[12]:

50% higher productivity

74% less stress

106% more energy at work

13% fewer sick days

76% more engagement

29% more satisfaction with their lives

40% less burnout

Trust arrives by foot and leaves by Ferrari.

Trust creates a competitive advantage.

Innovation happens at the speed of trust.

The more trust there is in an organization, the greater the exploration and exchange of ideas, the faster you can make those ideas reality, the higher the productivity.

"Hard" conversations—around budgets, accountability, weaknesses, and failures—suddenly become easier when there's trust. The faster you can get through those conversations, the faster you can get back to work and make change happen.

The two of us have met in person for a total of five minutes. Regardless, we decided to start a business together. Rooted in trust, we got through conversations about our business structure, ownership stakes, compensation, and investment all within a few hours, built a website in a few days, and launched our first pilot within a couple of months.

We talk about the speed of trust because we know personally how much better and faster work can be when trust is the engine.

You want to outpace your competitors? Build trust.

Highly successful performers in business and in sports show a level of trust and understanding that separates them from their competition.

—Pete Carroll

Trust is the basis of true belonging.

Belonging is different from fitting in.

True belonging is where you're able to be your authentic self without fear of lacking, punishment, or criticism. Fitting in is molding yourself to what the group thinks you should be.

True belonging starts with you, and it's difficult especially when, by and far, we're indoctrinated to fit in instead. From our first experience on a playground to our first day on the job, we're constantly immersed in systems and structures that incentivize fitting in.

Fitting in might help us navigate the early stages of connection, but over time, can leave us feeling unseen and disconnected. Ultimately, the cost of fitting in is relinquishing your identity to others. Belonging may be the harder route, but it's the path to deeper human connection and a strong sense of self paved in trust.

You can choose to go about your days looking for confirmation that you don't belong. If you do, you'll surely find it regardless if you're looking in a welcoming environment or a system of oppression.

Systems of oppression are never going to help you feel belonging, as they're designed to make you feel less than, excluded, or forced to give up parts of yourself to fit in, sometimes with your survival on the line.

While it may seem unfair, it's a necessity that you empower yourself to discover your own sense of belonging by choosing a different option.

You can choose to embrace all the edges that make you who you are and decide that you do belong. True belonging is only possible when you embrace that you are enough as you are and choose to trust yourself to be unapologetically you.

Once you find belonging in yourself, you can then choose to trust others to see and accept you as you are.

When you decide to show up with the vulnerability needed to share your true self with the world, you'll inspire others to do the same. By leading by example, you can help create the guardrails that make it increasingly safer for other people to make the same decision.

That is how the gift of choosing to belong can spread exponentially.

You Belo

NG HERE

-TRUST

If you don't trust yourself, how can you possibly get somebody else to trust you?

—Scott Perry

Trust is power.

Trust is the power to include and unleash.

Trust brings out the best in ourselves and in others—their energy, skills, talents, gifts, and ideas.

Trust is the basic element of cooperation; it forms the foundation for functioning relationships in organizations and communities.

When we engage in a trusted interaction, we aren't just more energized and effective. We also learn and grow more.

Trust is the power to build high-performing, inclusive teams that achieve remarkable results[13]. Trust is the power *within* yourself and *with* others.

Trust is the foundation for resilient leaders and organizations.

When facing a crisis or a period of uncertainty and significant change, some leaders will crumble under the pressure. The global COVID-19 pandemic disrupted life as we knew it, and with the necessary and rapid shift to remote work for many, we've seen the cracks in the old model of command-and-control and power-over-others become huge fractures in leadership and organizations.

Many organizations and entire industries have been upended and forced to adapt and sit in months of uncertainty. These challenging and ambiguous moments are the spotlights that reveal leadership[14].

In 2020, the global pandemic left the tourism and hospitality industry devastated as travel ground to a halt and many parts of the world were locked down.

Massimiliano Freddi, the founder and CEO of Wonderwood[15], an adventure park overlooking the picturesque Lake Maggiore in Italy, found himself co-creating a viable path forward with the help of his staff and community.

Freddi and his team had no guarantee this solution would work. Yet the trust in themselves, in one another, and in their guests saw Wonderwood through the challenges of 2020 with a successful season and no staff layoffs.

Trust provides a solid foundation for leaders in good times and bad, even and especially if you don't know what direction to move next. Trust gives rise to self-efficacy helping you rise up, move forward, and overcome difficulties.

Whether it's trust in oneself, one's team, or one's mission, trust is the bedrock for us to survive and even thrive in turbulent times.

Trust makes society resilient in times of uncertainty and adversity.

Trust strengthens our individual resilience and social fabric.

Humans are social creatures influenced by trusted social ties. Trusted and supportive relationships—personal and professional—are important factors in resilience[16], our ability to endure and navigate change and uncertainty. It's these trusted relationships that mobilize people to act. They're linked to greater psychological and physical wellbeing. They help us feel less stress when facing adversity.

Though we may be inclined to turn inwards when we're knocked down by hardship, wrapping yourself in the blanket of a trusted social fabric is a winning strategy to pick yourself up and adapt with strength.

Trust is the key to teamwork and winning collaboration.

Great teamwork isn't merely about doing your part of the work. Great team players bring out the best in their teammates and their team.

Without trust, we work around each other.

With trust, we work together. We enrich one another.

Collaboration is the foundation of the standard of living we enjoy today. Trust is the glue.

—Ram Charan

Trust begets trust.

Do you want to know the quickest way to build trust? (Of course you do.)

It's through extending trust first and being trustworthy. Surprise!

Inspire trust in others by trusting them as you would want them to trust you.

—Catherine Pulsifer

If you want to be trusted, you have to be trustworthy.

Trust is not a mythical thing. It's tangible and multifaceted.

Trust might seem like something that you just feel, but you can't put your finger on it. It might feel "fluffy" or "soft" or "woo-woo."

Trust is actually made up of a system of skills and competencies that, when developed, will lead you to becoming trustworthy.

The only way to build trust professionally or personally is by being trustworthy.

—Gerard Arpey

Act III - How to Build Trust

Trust has five facets.

We've developed a practical model to understand and assess trust in different contexts, and to build it. We call it the 5 Facets of Trust, and each facet covers a group of skills with actionable steps you can practice.

Here they are:

1. **Clarity**
2. **Credibility**
3. **Consistency**
4. **Caring**
5. **Connection**

See what we did there? They all start with the letter "C". Catchy, we know!

The formula isn't hard to remember, but the Facets aren't always easy to practice. They are, however, skills and competencies anyone can develop, regardless of where you're starting - if you put the work into it.

● ● ● ● ●

Trust is a skill learned over time so that, like a well-trained athlete, one makes the right moves, usually without much reflection.

—Robert C. Solomon

THE 5 FACETS OF TRUST

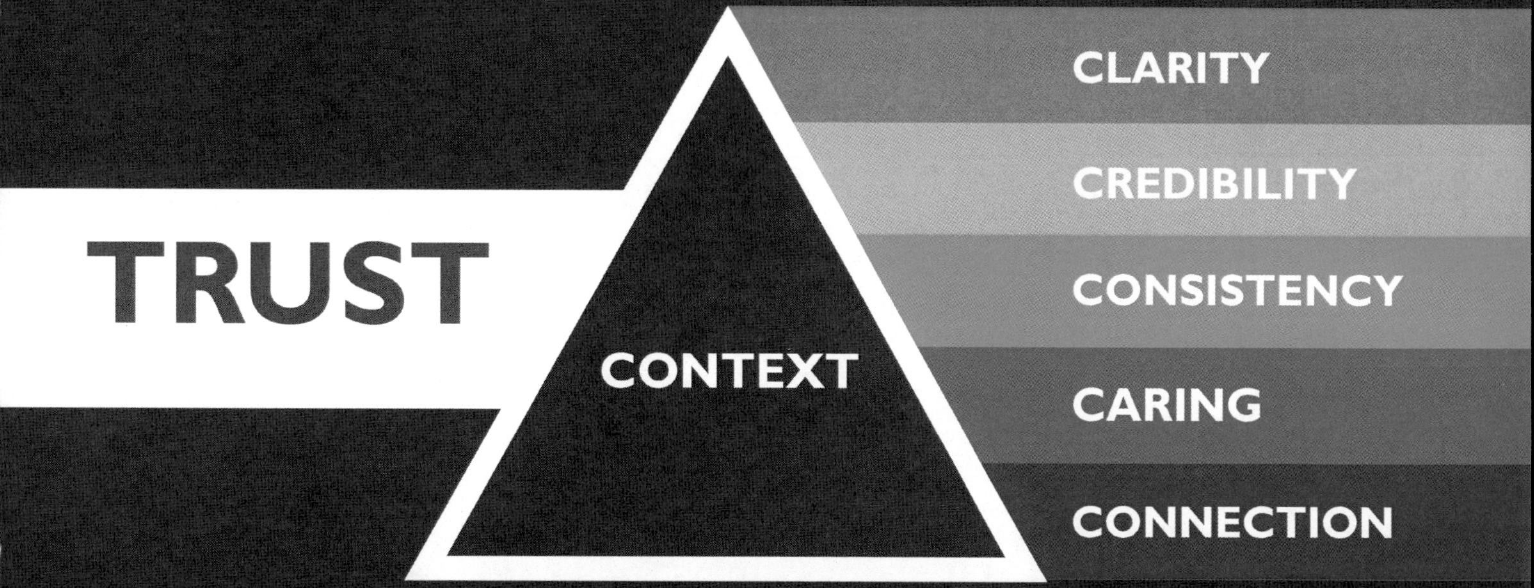

The First Facet of Trust: Clarity

Clarity is the quality of being clear and easy to understand.

Without clarity, your communications and intentions can be misunderstood. Attempts to show generosity can come off as greed, and credibility can come off as being insecure.

Clarity is the first facet because it is the foundation that underlies the rest.

To be credible you need to clearly demonstrate your credibility.

To be consistent you need to have clarity around why you're doing what you're doing.

To be caring you need to clearly demonstrate kindness, concern, and compassion for others.

To build connection you need to clearly understand and relate to the needs of others and communicate clearly.

Be clear.

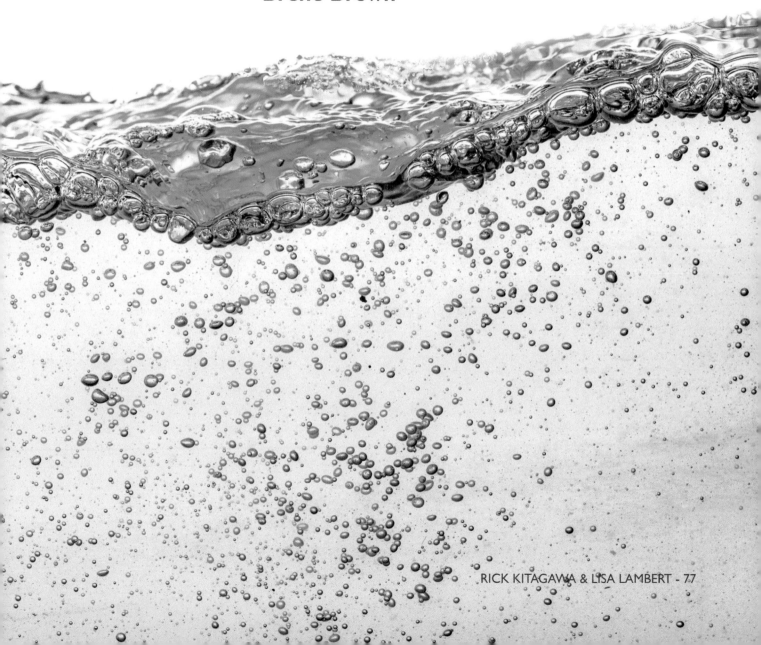

Clear is kind.

—Brené Brown

The Second Facet of Trust: Credibility

Credibility is the capacity or condition for belief.

Credibility is determined by what we call Credibility Signals. There are ten signals, and each one plays a part in your overall credibility regarding different areas of ability:

The 10 Credibility Signals

1. **Appearance:** How do I present myself to others?
2. **Charisma:** How well do I connect with others?
3. **Competency:** How well can I do the work?
4. **Evidence:** How can I demonstrate truth in my claim?
5. **Humility:** Do I set aside pride and hubris and show up with a sense of modesty, curiosity, and openness to learn?
6. **Integrity:** Do I act in accordance with my values?
7. **Relationships:** Who else trusts me?
8. **Reliability:** Do I get the job done consistently?
9. **Respectful:** Do I act with care and dignity towards others?
10. **Truthfulness:** Am I honest, even when it's hard or inconvenient?

Credibility signals are the easiest to focus on when building trust, but are also one of the quickest areas in which you can lose trust as well.

A good leader is probably no different in any culture in the sense that a good leader must have credibility. That is something one establishes... based on the way one handles himself and by his established track record.

—Dr. Victor K. Fung

The Third Facet of Trust: Consistency

Consistency is the harmony of behavior, narrative, process, parts, and/or features.

As we said earlier, credibility is what often gets focused on, but in the pursuit of trust, credibility crumbles quickly if each signal is focused on as a one-off.

Consistency is doing what you say, acting in a dependable way in a variety of situations, and being true to the image you project out into the world. It's done repeatedly, and over time.

Consistency is the repeated effort of nurturing your trust plant. It's habits and actions repeated again and again. It's like the scientific method: repeat an experiment multiple times, and if the results all stay the same, then you can believe those results to be true.

Consistency is also very fragile. It needs to be built up over time, yet a single lapse can be incredibly damaging to trust.

A surgeon who has thousands of successful surgeries only needs to sew a scalpel up into a patient once to lose trust.

A leader who has been known for their commitment to diversity and inclusion only has to get caught once making an off-the-cuff racist, misogynistic, or homophobic "joke" to lose trust.

Consistency demands discipline, and it's powerful when it's been built up, drip by drip.

Trust is built with consistency.

—Lincoln Chafee

The Fourth Facet of Trust: Caring

Caring is the feeling and demonstration of kindness, concern, and compassion for others.

Small, consistent acts of genuine care can make a big difference. Showing care for others is one of the quickest ways to build trust and is extremely powerful, but if faked, can be the most unforgivable betrayal.

Even if someone is highly competent, if we are not convinced that they care about us and have our best interests in mind, then we're not going to trust them. Often, those that are competent but don't seem to care are those we dislike and distrust.

It's easy to pretend or say that we care, but if we're not genuine or we don't demonstrate care, it's easy to make things worse by coming off as phoney. The easiest way to actually care? Start by getting curious about others.

Ask how they're doing and actually listen to them—don't just listen for them to stop talking. Separate this act from checking up on a project or their work and check in on them as a human more than you check up. Consider how you might add value to them.

Demonstrating care doesn't have to be expensive, like giving customers massive promotional discounts or spending hours in one-on-one meetings with an employee. It can be as simple as remembering and using your customer's name, or genuinely thanking your employee for a specific contribution. It could be sending a friend their favorite baked good on their birthday, or remembering to order the gluten-free, vegan option for a colleague at every company meal.

These can sometimes feel like little things, but they're things that when done consistently add up and make people feel deeply cared about.

When we feel cared for, we can feel psychologically safe, and this extension of vulnerability is what most human connection—and trust—is based upon.

People don't care how much you know until they know how much you care.

—Theodore Roosevelt

The Fifth Facet of Trust: Connection

Connection is the act of relating to and building relationships with others.

Connection is the natural progression from caring about others. By caring, we make it easier for people to choose to care about us, and this bond is what relationships are built upon.

Connection requires us to reach out to those we seek to build trust with. It's built with a compilation of some of the most revered leadership skills: charisma, storytelling, public speaking, decision making, direct communication, etc.

Connection is the ability to stand on a stage and make the audience want to talk to you after you finish your presentation. It's being able to deliver bad news and be thanked for your transparency and care. It's articulating who it is for, as well as who it is not for, and why it matters.

Connection is building the relationships that allow us to grow and scale up to the change that we want to make in the world.

We show our trust in the way that we show up for each other, the way that we communicate together, the way that we work together to maintain a friendship. Every opportunity we have to do that and show up and do that builds trust and it's like putting money in the bank – it's like a savings account of trust.

—Kat Vellos

Being trustworthy is a weakest link issue.

You're only as trustworthy as the strength of your weakest Facet of Trust.

You could have built and sold several successful multi-million dollar ventures, but if you don't show that you care about my company's best interests, I'll look to someone else as a trusted business advisor.

Maybe you graduated from a prestigious medical school and consistently save people's lives. But if you're unclear on why I need to take a specific action, I might listen to search engine medical advice instead.

In any given situation, your weakest Facet of Trust is the basis of how much you're going to be trusted.

Trust is like the air we breathe—when it's present, nobody really notices; when it's absent, everybody notices.

—**Warren Buffett**

Our trustworthiness is contextual.

When it comes to trust, like most things, context matters.

Perhaps you're my loving parent who's raised me all of these years, but if you've never completed an electrical circuit before, I'm going to trust the five-star electrician I hired when I need to rewire my ceiling fan.

We need to remember that while we might be a trusted expert in some fields, we're not trusted experts in everything. Different contexts can shift us from highly trusted to trust-less, so it's imperative that we put in the effort to understand the points of view of those we seek to build trust with and do so with humility and respect.

● ● ● ● ● ● ● ● ● ● ● ● ● ● ● ●

The best way to build trust is in 3D.

The 5 Facets of Trust are applied across the 3 Dimensions of Trust:

1. **Trust with yourself**
2. **Trust with another**
3. **Trust at scale**

When it comes to the 3 Dimensions of Trust, the whole is greater than the sum of its parts. Each of the 3 Dimensions needs to be enriched so they can act together to harness the full potential of trust.

BUILDING TRUST IN 3D

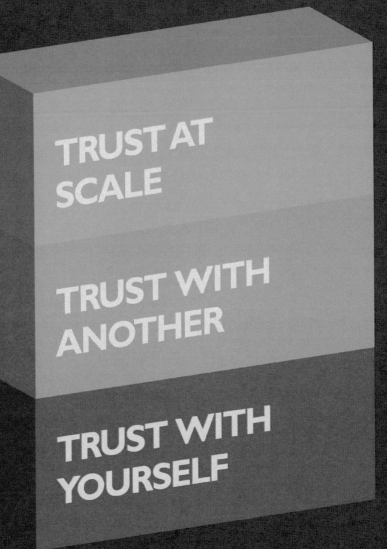

TRUST AT SCALE

TRUST WITH ANOTHER

TRUST WITH YOURSELF

The First Dimension of Trust: Self-trust is the bedrock.

Trusting in ourselves is the foundation of all trust.

Self-trust is not about trusting in yourself to have all the answers. Rather, it's about cultivating a solid and caring relationship with yourself and trusting that you'll be able to navigate whatever comes your way.

Our self-trust influences how we show up in the world and how we choose to place our trust in the people and things around us. Our self-trust helps us discern when to rely on our intuition and when to rely on broader insights.

Lack of self-trust is common even though it's limiting.

When we don't trust in ourselves, we operate in a mentality of lack, doubt, regret, and fear. When we don't have a strong relationship with ourselves and trust in ourselves, it's challenging to build strong, trusting relationships with others. Low self-trust is often at the core of leaders grasping for control, pulling things close and micromanaging. Low self-trust leads us to close ourselves in, rather than opening up and stepping into possibility.

By opening up into an expansive posture, we're able to make space to more freely extend trust to ourselves and others. We position ourselves to gracefully navigate the tension between humility and ego so we can stand firmly with a measured amount of confidence and make space to generously connect and care for people while leaning into uncertainty. This expansive posture is one that builds credibility and trust rapidly, as well as acts as the basis for more resilient leaders, teams, and organizations.

A way we can build and strengthen our foundation of self-trust is through small, consistent actions. This back-to-basics approach can propel us along the journey of trusting in ourselves and cementing the foundation of new habits that highlight our strengths and shore up our weaknesses.

What makes it challenging for you to fully trust yourself? What small thing could you do today to start building self-trust?

Think about a goal you have, and work back to the smallest step that would move you forward.

Do you want to write a book? Start by practicing writing for five or ten minutes a day.

Looking to build more connection with your team? Write one person an email focused on what you value about them and their work.

Want to improve your public speaking skills? Start by saying yes to the small things, like speaking up when someone asks if anyone would like to share something in a meeting.

While sometimes you may need the lift that comes from others trusting in you more than you trust in yourself, building trust with yourself doesn't come from external validation. Nor is it about making huge, monumental shifts.

Self-trust comes from within and is built up through the consistency of taking small actions. Then you can begin to trust that you can do larger and larger actions.

The best place to start bolstering the fullness of trust is by building and strengthening trust with yourself. Build a strong foundation for the house, and it'll last the test of time.

If we don't trust ourselves to bring our own unique perspective and abilities to a problem, then how are we going to trust others to do the same?

–Mike Lyndon

The Second Dimension of Trust: Thrive by building trust with another.

The core of human interaction is one-on-one relationships.

No person ever goes it alone. You might be the one atop the podium with the medal, the celebrated CEO, or standing on the stage delivering a TED Talk, but everything requires relationships: past, present, and future.

You need the organizers of the event, the coach, the teammates, the administrators, the marketers, the employees. You even need your competition—competitors push you to greater heights.

There is a myth of the individual contributor or lone genius that undermines the necessity of all of the other people who make success happen, and let's fully discard that myth now.

Thriving is a team sport. We need other people.

And to get their support, their enrollment, their collaboration, we need relationships based on trust.

You're reading this book for a reason, so you're probably seeking to build and strengthen trust. When you're looking to build trust with others, you'll need others to build it with.

Think back to that goal you were considering in the last chapter. As you're building trust with yourself, who might have the skill set, knowledge, or support that could help accelerate you towards your goal?

Consider who you might need to enroll to make your goal a reality. Do you need your teammates, customers, board, or CEO's buy-in to get this project off the ground?

Does your friend's brother's husband own a business like the one you want to build?

Might your cousin know someone who teaches web design?

Who might help you be able to reach out for support in furthering your cause?

Given what you now know, how might you build trust with them?

The only relationships in this world that have ever been worthwhile and enduring have been those in which one person could trust another.

–Samuel Smiles

The Third Dimension of Trust: Navigate complexity by building trust at scale.

Systems based on human interaction—like organizations, society, culture, and economics—tend to be complex.

While complex systems are difficult to model and predict, they can still be infused with behaviors, processes, systems, and patterns of interaction that engender trust.

Building trust at scale requires leaders to master the basics and consider all the pieces of the trust puzzle. It involves developing all the 5 Facets of Trust and practicing every skill in your Trust-Centered Leader's toolkit.

It's also about truly stepping into the expansive posture of a Trust-Centered Leader that helps other leaders to shine and shine brighter, establishing a high-trust culture. It's building a system of trust that supports and is supported by all parties involved, and operates with minimal oversight, bureaucratic theatre, and red tape.

Many people bristle at the thought of introducing new systems and procedures; at the potential they'll have to overcome more bureaucratic hurdles that will impede on their effectiveness, creativity, or autonomy. However not all systems have to be rigid, unyielding, or based on new technology.

Strong systems that engender trust can be flexible, iterative, human-centered, and made of simple building blocks. For example, in our work we've found that teams and organizations build much stronger and resilient cultural foundations when they go beyond values by making and being accountable to a succinct co-created set of community agreements[17]. These are a great way to build up that system of trust that operates smoothly and effectively with little oversight.

Community agreements are a concise set of shared and clear commitments about how we are going to show up as leaders and teammates. They're a tool to activate community identity by thoughtfully shaping group dynamics, patterns of interaction, and collective conversation. They involve setting clear expectations, making promises and keeping them—a practical approach that helps build trust at scale and is reinforced by a self-sustaining system that supports community members with leaders seldom needing to police.

One of the key aspects of community agreements is that they're co-created. This helps all members of the community to feel a sense of ownership of the agreements and to see themselves in them. While it can be tempting to present a ready-made set of agreements, take the time to slow down and get input from all parties involved.

And remember, if you and your team are new to this tool, give yourself a chance to pilot it on a small scale and learn from the experience. Instead of starting by rolling out community agreements across your organization, consider testing them out in the context of a recurring meeting or a small project. You can iterate and scale from there.

Building trust at scale makes organizations and communities better, and we need people like you to learn how to do it and do it well.

Creation = vulnerable generative action
Co-creation = mutually vulnerable generative action

–Steve Frost

Trust is the most significant predictor of individuals' satisfaction within their organizations.

–Jim Kouzes and Barry Posner

Trust can enable action, but action ultimately creates trust.

The unfortunate way of the world is that often we wait for trust in order to make it safe for us to take action. On the surface, this makes sense: sometimes our survival depends on it, and we don't want to put our fate in the hands of those we don't trust. However, oftentimes we need to act "as if" and take action in order for us to earn the trust needed to move forward.

Additionally, we often think that leadership or building trust is about "saying the right thing." Talk is cheap without follow-thru. As a leader you are judged by the congruency between what you say and what you do. Remember the trust puzzle. People judge you on the congruency and consistency of your words and deeds.

Do you fulfill your promises?

Do you show caring not just when it's convenient or easy or with your favorite team members?

Do you tell the truth when it benefits you as well as when it doesn't?

Do you honor your values when it comes to making hard decisions?

We judge people based on what they do, and if you want to be judged as trustworthy, then you've got to take trustworthy actions.

It's important to reassess trust so we can trust wisely.

It's important that we give our trust to those deserving of it. That involves challenging our own implicit and systemic biases that might lead us to withholding trust from the trustworthy or to extend it to the untrustworthy.

Once we've made a decision to trust, we seldom revisit it. That can be perilous in our fast-paced world.

While a person or organization might have been trustworthy at one time, that may no longer be true. While we ourselves might have been trustworthy at one time, that may no longer be the case.

Trust is a choice to be made in each moment.

With what you know now, how might you reassess who and what you trust in?

With what you know now, how might others reassess their trust in you?

You can never build too much trust.

Being trusted is a journey, not a final destination or achievement to be celebrated. If you're already trusted? Fantastic! And, like a plant, you need to continuously nurture trust in your relationships.

In our consulting practice we teach trust, and we're constantly working to level up our own trustworthiness. There is no risk of ever being too trusted.

That said, remember the danger in abusing trust. Trust is powerful, but fragile, and abuses of trust are difficult to repair.

If you want to become trusted, the clearest path is to become trustworthy. Literally, to become worthy of being trusted.

Becoming a Trust-Centered Leader who earns and is worthy of trust is a consistent practice. It's upskilling yourself in all 5 Facets and all 3 Dimensions of Trust. It's a commitment to being the type of person who can drive change and can sleep well on a pillow of integrity, respect, and trust.

Trust is a choice: it's something you choose to earn and extend and others choose to extend to you.

While earning trust is not guaranteed, choosing to show up and lead in a way that is trustworthy and deserving of trust is the highest reward risk you can take, regardless of the outcome.

Our world needs you to make the choice only you can make.

Will you make the decision to build a more trustworthy and trusted world with us?

We trust that you will.

Epilogue

Trust opens up new and
unimagined possibilities.

—Robert C. Solomon

We're trusting you.

As management guru Peter Drucker aptly said, "The best way to predict the future is to create it."

Too many people feel disconnected, isolated, lonely, or like they don't belong. And it doesn't have to be this way.

The future is trust.

The only way to create a better, more inclusive world is to build a more trustworthy one full of benevolent, generous leaders. You know, people like you.

Want a more trusted world? Then build it.

The future is you.

110 - THE FUTURE IS TRUST

Download the Group Discussion Guide and Discover Additional Trust-Centered Resources

Knowledge is different than know-how. To help you integrate the lessons from *The Future Is Trust* into your own Trust-Centered Leadership practice, go even deeper on specifics topics explored in the book, and engage in transformative conversations about trust, we invite you to visit:

TheFutureIsTrust.com

There you can:
- Get a free 25-question Group Discussion Guide plus facilitation tips to help catalyze a thought-provoking conversation with your team or book club members
- Sign up for our weekly newsletter where we share practical Trust-Centered insights and exercises to help you level-up your leadership
- Get additional practical resources to help you earn, extend, strengthen, and even restore trust

We also invite you to listen to the *In Trust* podcast on your favorite podcast player. In this weekly podcast, Rick and Lisa share stories, practical insights, and deep-dive conversations with special guests all about—you guessed it—trust. Learn more about the *In Trust* podcast at **spotlighttrust.com/podcast**

References

1. Six Sigma. 2017. "Vitality 2017: Finding the Value of Emotions in the Global Workforce." Research: Organizational Vitality 2017. http://www.6seconds.org/2017/07/23/vital-organization-key-findings/.

2. Wikipedia contributors. 2021. "Elizabeth Holmes." Wikipedia, The Free Encyclopedia. https://en.wikipedia.org/wiki/Elizabeth_Holmes.

3. Wikipedia contributors. 2021. "Theranos." Wikipedia, The Free Encyclopedia. https://en.wikipedia.org/w/index.php?title=Theranos&oldid=1000559442.

4. Edmondson, Amy. 1999. "Psychological Safety and Learning Behavior in Work Teams." Administrative Science Quarterly 44, no. 2 (June): 350-383. 2666999.

5. Dweck, Carol S., and Ellen L. Leggett. 1988. "A Social-Cognitive Approach to Motivation and Personality." Psychological Review 95, no. 2 (April): 256-273.

6. Pew Research Center. 2020. "Social trust in advanced economies is lower among young people and those with less education." Factank. https://www.pewresearch.org/fact-tank/2020/12/03/social-trust-in-advanced-economies-is-lower-among-young-people-and-those-with-less-education/.

7. Willoughby, A. R., J. A. Barraza, H. Javitz, B. J. Roach, M. de Zambotti, M. T. Harrison, J. C. Cox, et al. 2016. "Electrophysiological and neuroendocrine correlates of trust in the investment game." Journal of Intelligence Community Research & Development., (December). Unknown.

8. Zak, Paul J. 2017. "The Neuroscience of Trust." Harvard Business Review. https://hbr.org/2017/01/the-neuroscience-of-trust.

9. Feldman, R., M. Monakhov, M. Pratt, and R. P. Ebstein. 2016. "Oxytocin Pathway Genes: Evolutionary Ancient System Impacting on Human Affiliation, Sociality, and

Psychopathology." Biological Psychiatry 79, no. 3 (February): 174-84. 10.1016/j. biopsych.2015.08.008.

10. Savolainen, T., and S. Häkkinen. 2011. "Trusted to Lead: Trustworthiness and its Impact on Leadership." Open Source Business Resource, (March). http://timreview.ca/article/429.

11. Trust Across America. 2020. "Trust: The Business Case for CEOs & Boards." Trust Across America-Trust Around the World. https://www.trustacrossamerica.com/blog/?p=4947.

12. Zak, Paul J. 2017. "The Neuroscience of Trust." Harvard Business Review. https://hbr.org/2017/01/the-neuroscience-of-trust.

13. Hakanen, M., and A. Soudunsaari. 2012. "Building Trust in High-Performing Teams." Technology Innovation Management Review, 2, no. 6 (June): 38-41. 10.22215.

14. Bennis, W., and R. J. Thomas. 2002. "Crucibles of Leadership." Harvard Business Review. https://hbr.org/2002/09/crucibles-of-leadership.

15. Wonderwood. n.d. "Wonderwood." Wonderwood. Accessed January 15, 2021. https://www.wonderwood.it/.

16. Ozbay, F., D. C. Johnson, E. Dimoulas, C. A. Morgan, D. Charney, and S. Southwick. 2007. "Social support and resilience to stress: from neurobiology to clinical practice." Psychiatry 4, no. 5 (May): 35-40. https://www.ncbi.nlm.nih.gov/pmc/articles/PMC2921311/pdf/PE_4_5_35.pdf.

17. Spotlight Trust. 2021. "Organizational Values Often Fall Short, So Co-Create Community Agreements." Spotlight Trust. https://spotlighttrust.com/organizational-values-often-fall-short-so-co-create-community-agreements.

Links are accurate at time of publication.

Photo Credits

All uncredited photos sourced from Canva.
p.7 - Niv Rozenberg - https://unsplash.com/@nivroz
p.12 - Dave Hoefler - https://unsplash.com/@johnwestrock
p.14 - JP Valery - https://unsplash.com/@jpvalery
p.16 - Chase Wilson - https://unsplash.com/@jiggliemon
p.19 - Blake Weyland - https://unsplash.com/@blakeweyland
p.21 - Ekaterina Bolovtsova - https://www.pexels.com/@ekaterina-bolovtsova
p.26 - Chuttersnap - https://unsplash.com/@chuttersnap
p.28 - Giorgio Trovato - https://unsplash.com/@giorgiotrovato
p.31 - Willi Heidelbach - https://pixabay.com/users/wilhei-883152
p.32 - Rudy and Peter Skitterians - https://pixabay.com/users/skitterphoto-324082
p.33 - Julia Maior - https://unsplash.com/@juliamaior
p.34 - eslfuntaiwan - https://pixabay.com/users/eslfuntaiwan-415390
p.37 - Armin Rimoldi - https://www.pexels.com/@armin-rimoldi
p.38 - Olia Danilevich - https://www.pexels.com/@olia-danilevich
p.40 - Gabriel Jimenez - https://unsplash.com/@gabrielj_photography
p.41 - Matthias Bertelli - https://www.pexels.com/@bertellifotografia
p.44,45 - Federico Beccari - https://unsplash.com/@federize
p.48 - Hoang Loc - https://www.pexels.com/@hoang-loc-748820
p.52 - Rodolfo Quiros - https://www.pexels.com/@rquiros?
p.55 - Martin Katler - https://unsplash.com/@martinkatler
p.62 - Sam Kolder - https://www.pexels.com/@samkolder
p.64,65 - Tobias - https://unsplash.com/@tbshg
p.68 - Polina Tankilevitch - https://www.pexels.com/@polina-tankilevitch
p.69 - Alan Mas - https://www.pexels.com/@allan-mas
p.72,73 - Theme Inn - https://unsplash.com/@themeinn
p.83, 93 - Karolina Grabowska - https://www.pexels.com/@karolina-grabowska
p.87 - Steve Halama - https://unsplash.com/@steve3p_0
p.90,91 - Guillaume Bergaglia - https://unsplash.com/@guillaume_br
p.98,99 - Joseph Phillips - https://www.pexels.com/@joseph-phillips-2044494
p.106,107 - Jayson Delos Santos - https://www.pexels.com/@dsnsyj

Acknowledgements

We are incredibly grateful and humbled by the abundance of support, feedback, and encouragement we received from our families, friends, clients, colleagues, collaborators, and community members that proved instrumental in the writing, editing, and shipping of this book. Proper thanks would fill a whole other book! Our aim with this book was to get to the point, and we're carrying that theme forward in these Acknowledgements. That said, we want to acknowledge that bringing this book to life took a village. To all our trusted villagers, thank you: we could not have done this without you.

Our profound thanks to a person who likely doesn't know the extent of the role he played in nudging us to write this book sooner rather than later, Dean Karrell - thank you for your kindness, wisdom, and encouragement.

We want to give special thanks to everyone who so generously gave us their time, energy, and attention to riff on concepts, participate in pilot programs where we iterated on frameworks we share in the book, and review early drafts: Graham Ballachey, William "Batch" Batchelder, Bob Bonniol, Marcelo Cury, Mark Danylchuk, Steve Danylchuk, Shane Delaney, Covington Doan, Ryan Flahive, Massimiliano Freddi, Steve Frost, Jamie Kirwin, Travis Martin, Emily McArdle, Sari Meline, Eric Moeller, Tyler Murdoch, Selena Ng, Shenuri Nugawila, Sara Leth Ottosen, Scott Perry, Stacy Richards, Helen Sanderson, Ian Scott, Peter Shepherd, Eve Skylar, Colin Steele, Yash Tekriwal, Jade Waterman, Shannon Weber, and Richard Wells. You provided us with such thoughtful feedback and we hope you can see the impact you've had on this book. As Rick always says, "Teamwork makes the dream work," and you helped bring this dream of ours to life while making it better.

To the Name Whisperer herself Louise Karch, we hope you see the influence of your word wizardry in our work.

To our fearless, flexible, and thorough proofreader and editor Al Gilliom, thank you for keeping our office managers (Lisa's dogs) enchanted with your piano magic while going above and beyond in scrutinizing every word and sentence of this book to ensure we published something coherent and readable.

To Aray M. Till, thank you for lending us your keen eyes and preventing our bumbling layout designer (Rick) from creating a monstrous catastrophe.

To Carra Simpson, thank you for sharing your abundant knowledge of the world of publishing with us and holding us by the hand at times to ensure we managed to navigate our way through it.

To the altMBA and Akimbo community members, thank you for sharing your magic with us and your insatiable desire to learn and level-up. To our coach peers: we felt the support of the Grove throughout the publication process and we're grateful to not only call you colleagues, but dear friends. To Seth Godin, Alex Peck, Marie Schacht, Wes Kao, and Kelli Wood: thank you for creating a bold and transformative space for us to first collide and kick off our international collaboration even though we are physically separated by an international border and live 1,281 miles/ 2,062 kilometres apart.

Leaders can't lead without a team, and we'd like to give special thanks to our families who have supported us through thick and thin. Eve, Tim, Bebop, Rocksteady, and Mochi - we are forever grateful and you inspire us to show up and give our best every day. To our parents and our brothers, you were the first ones to teach us about leadership and the first ones to trust in us before we even knew the word. Thank you for your trust and your teachings, especially in those times when we took our time to learn.

Huge thanks to everyone who has been walking alongside us since the early days, and for those that continue to trust us to this day. Your fellowship and trust mean more to us than you'll ever know.

RiSa (Rick + Lisa)
Pasadena, CA United States + North Vancouver, BC, Canada
May 2021

About Spotlight Trust

Co-founded and co-led by Rick Kitagawa and Lisa Lambert, Spotlight Trust is an organizational design and leadership development partner that helps organizations harness the power of trust to become more human, creative, adaptive, and effective.

Our approach is rooted in our practical frameworks for earning, strengthening, and even restoring trust, which make up the foundation for what we call Trust-Centered Leadership™.

Our frameworks enable relevant, dynamic, inclusive, and continuous learning and development that supports organizations, leaders, and teams to anticipate, prepare, and adapt to the only internal and external constant: change.

Learn more about Spotlight Trust and sign up for our weekly newsletter at **www.spotlighttrust.com**

About the Authors

 **Rick Kitagawa** (he/him/his) is a consultant, executive coach, and facilitator that has worked with executives, founders, creatives, and leaders from around the globe and Fortune 50 companies. Past clients include leaders at Apple, Google, Starbucks, Warby Parker, Citigroup, and Gap, Inc. As a top-rated university lecturer, he has helped thousands of creatives turn their passions into thriving careers in hyper-competitive industries.

Rick also spends his time as a Head Coach for the altMBA and Akimbo workshops, creating spaces of belonging for youth at Codebreakers, producing the *Inner Monster Podcast*, co-hosting the *In Trust* podcast, and writing daily newsletters about leadership, organizational design and culture, creativity, and current events.

Rick is an award-winning visual artist and writer and is one of the best Skee-Ball rollers in the world (seriously). He also really, really likes monsters and is based in Pasadena, CA, USA on the ancestral land of the Kizh/Gabrieleño people.

Learn more about Rick and sign up for his newsletter at rickkitagawa.com and connect on LinkedIn at linkedin.com/in/rickkitagawa

Lisa Lambert (she/her/hers) is a consultant, executive coach, and award-winning facilitator with a passion for innovation. She's worked with executives, organizations, multidisciplinary teams, and leaders who are tackling complex problems and driving transformational endeavors on all seven continents. Lisa enjoys transforming chaos into order (with plenty of room for improv) and has shaped strategy, communications, and organizational design for world-leading projects that have raised over $500 million in public and private investment.

Lisa also serves as a Head Coach for the altMBA and Akimbo workshops, co-hosts the *In Trust* podcast, mentors young entrepreneurs through YELL Canada, and writes a daily newsletter about leadership, innovation, collaboration, and culture.

Lisa lives in North Vancouver, BC, Canada, the unceded territories of the xʷməθkʷəy̓əm (Musqueam), Sḵwx̱wú7mesh (Squamish), and Səl̓íl̓witulh (Tsleil-Waututh) Nations. You can often find Lisa running the North Shore trails with her two dogs, discovering a new winding road on two wheels, or dreaming about her next scuba diving adventure.

Learn more about Lisa and sign up for her newsletter at lisalambert.online and connect on LinkedIn at linkedin.com/in/lmlambert

Made in the USA
Monee, IL
22 July 2021